IMPORTANT

It should be noted here that the author takes no issue with or casts any aspirations upon either the alcohol beverage industry or the pharmaceutical industry – none! The target audience of this book and it's content is the struggling alcoholic & addict who continues to have difficulty maintaining their sobriety. That and nothing more!

The stories in this book and it's contents are offered for the consideration of those alcoholics and addicts who continue to have difficulty maintaining their sobriety and for anyone else who is interested in the subject.

The entire content is only offered for the consideration of the reader and nothing in this book should be construed as diagnosis of any thing; treatment of any kind, medical anything of any kind for anyone. Nothing should be construed as advise but rather of interest to the reader. In essence this book was written to encourage the reader to seek treatment for their alcoholism and drug addiction.

Nothing presented in this book is intended to nor does it in any way discredit any other resource. This simply represents an additional resource for those struggling alcoholics and addicts to see if it might be of interest and or help to them.

1

Acknowlegements

First and foremost, to my heavenly Father for his gift of Jesus Christ, my Lord and Savior, and through him for the many blessings and miracles that have been bestowed upon my life.

To my parents; my mother who nurtured me and my father who gave me wisdom and an excellent set of work ethics and noble values by which I live my life today!

To Patty, the love of my life through who's eyes God smiled upon the earth.

To Chris, a friend of many years who was there for me in times of trouble in my life.

To my friend and sidekick "Cowboy Kev", who to this day remains the best friend any man could ever want.

To Pastor Bill who was the officient at my ordination and was the kindest most gentle man that I was privileged to know and also to his son Nick who helped me on the mission field when he was a boy and who, to this day, plays a major role in my life.

To George Benedict and Mark Eply of the Seafield Center Alcohol and Drug Treatment Center in Westhampton Beach New York who gave me a position on the staff doing what I was born to do; Pastoral Counselor presenting seminars on life that have touched and helped the lives of many thousands of alcoholics and addicts.

To Stacy, a friend whom I truly love and who's help in so many areas of my life has made a difference.

To Tina, who gave me a home when I was homeless and years later to Jackie, who worked so hard to keep the house, the taxes and the other bills so costly but kept the rent low for me during the lean years so I would have a place to live.

To my daughters, of who I am so proud, Elizabeth, who is an RN, and Cathy who is studying to be a First Surgical Assistant and to both my sons, Paul and Craig, who have gone to be with God.

To my dear friend Billy, a true genius in his own right, a one of a kind tech guy with a heart as big as the world.

And others too numereous to mention.

There were rough times in my life, the loss of my wealth, my home, my family, homeless years, and Patty, the love of my life who died at 42 years old on October 16, 1982. I miss her to this day.

Through it all the angels of God feathered the blows and today, at 90 years old I stand tall and have written this book as part of my ministry. I am grateful to all those people and in all those things that I have mentioned here and for the many miracles and blessings have been bestowed upon my life that there isn't room enough to list.

Forward

On a cold day in 1997, I was introduced to the Reverend Fred Valdes. We were walking into the rehab center for whom we both worked-he, for over seven years at that point, and me for just a couple of weeks. He introduced himself to me as we entered the building and I to him. I introduced myself as a brand new "counselor" and new to the field. He quickly invited me to sit in on his afternoon workshop. As luck would have it, my timing was perfect-he would be starting his workshop shortly after my meeting would end! I really did not know who he was, but I could tell that he was held in high regard by everyone we encountered as we walk through the hallway. The Reverend had a presence and a professional respect that I hoped to one day Garner.

You could hear a pin drop; he had command of the audience. I was thoroughly impressed and wondered would people listen to me the way they did to him? It was clear to me that from that moment on that "The Rev" (as all of his longtime colleagues and clients referred to him) was making his life work about Reaching Out to Alcoholics and Addicts...those for whom maintaining sobriety was not difficult and others who would continue to have difficulty maintaining their sobriety.

I feverishly took notes that day and amongst other lessons, learned that "two dead batteries can't start a car"-something to this day I share with anyone who would benefit! So many valuable lessons taken from The Rev's treasure trove. I find myself mentoring others the same way he did me and others... an opportunity I do not take lightly.

Twenty three and a half years have passed since our chance meeting in the parking lot and I hope that I have grown into the that professional I imagined I could become. I find myself repeating "Rev-isms". The Rev has been a mentor for so many recovering people and professionals. This book embodies who he is... never giving up hope, helping people let go of the past, and instilling hope for all no matter how hopelessly they may feel their lives have become.

This book is a gift from The Rev's heart and I hope that all who read it will pass it along to anyone who is ready for The Rev's message!

Anita Marie Young, LCSW-R, BCD

Nothing in this book is intended
to discredit any other source.
This book represents an addition
to the existing pool of resources.
It enables the alcoholic and addict who
continues to have difficulty maintaining
their sobriety to see things from
another angle;
i.e. expressed in another way.

"Outside The Box"

I offer this in an effort to help
those alcoholics and addicts
who have difficulty maintaining
their sobriety with stability

Fountains Of Understanding

OF CONSIDERABLE IMPORTANCE
Nothing in this book constitutes diagnosis,
treatment, or medical anything of any kind
for anyone and should not be construed as such.
It's content is not meant to diagnose,
treat, or cure anything.
This book offers "outside the box" concepts
to see if they can ignite the spark for serious and
involved participation in treatment for those alcoholics
and addicts who continue to have difficulty maintaining
their sobriety. The content of this book is only offered
for the consideration of that target audience in an effort
to help them achieve stable sobriety.

Along with Addiction
there are sometimes other factors of a Medical
or Psychological nature involved and so
the following may be appropriate:
Diagnosis and treatment by specific
qualified healthcare providors.

Help is available
through any one of or a combination of
any of the following as circumstances dictate
to deal with Addiction: AA, NA, Rehab, TC,
and perhaps the addition of other programs
that are appropriate.

Fountains Of Understanding

When you show someone
something from another angle
they see it from another angle
and they usually say
"wow, I never looked at it that way".

That change in perception
can enable someone
to change the direction
of their life.

If your life is going in the
wrong direction this book
shows you how making a
change is within reach.

ONE SIZE DOES NOT FIT ALL
and so...

It just makes sense to show things from another angle i.e.

"OUTSIDE THE BOX"

To help those who can benefit from a little more help

If in your heart...

you really do seek understanding
and answers in order to change the direction
of your life, then what's in this book may help
you to find the understanding and the
answers that you are looking for.

Fountains Of Understanding

The Excitement Of The "Hustle And The Chase"

This actually took place in a workshop that I was conducting in a rehab many years ago with an audience of alcoholics and addicts, men and women of all ages.

Lots of mommys and daddys in the audience along with many other men and women of all ages. All listened to the exchange that follows here. Most in attendance had been in and out of rehabs, AA and or NA, some in and out of jail and they continue to have difficulty maintaining their sobriety. Addiction knows no bounds.

The Hustle And The Chase

She was a woman around 30 years old and stood up in a workshop that I was conducting in the rehab...

She said "I'm not gonna use alcohol and drugs anymore but, I don't want to give up the Hustle and the Chase. I love the excitement of it! You know that I want my children back. They are in foster care".

I said; "I don't think you can have the Hustle and the Chase and your children too because with the Hustle and the Chase comes the alcohol and drugs".

Then She said; "**You have to understand!** I'm not gonna use Alcohol and Drugs! I'm gonna go to meetings! I'm gonna get a sponsor and do all the things they say I should do".
Again, she said ; " **You have to understand!** Im just not going to use alcohol and drugs but I can't live without the Hustle and the Chase. If you take that away from me I will be in an emotional cage."

I gently replied to her statement...
"**You can't take the alcohol or drugs out of the** *Hustle and the Chase and the excitement that goes with it anymore than you can take the wet out of the water".*
Read That Again

11

I said; "If you want the *Hustle and the Chase* and the fact that the <u>drugs and alcohol come with the Hustle and the Chase</u>, you may not be able to have your two little girls back"

"There's the possibility that you can't have them *back* **because it seems that you want to do, what you want to do at their expense."**

She said; **"What do you mean at their expense? I love my children! I want them with me!"**

I Challenged Her!

I said; "Maybe you don't love your children."

She angrily said; **"Don't you tell me that I don't love my children!"**

I said, **"The Evidence Of Love is in Behavior.** The Behavior Of Love is such that you make the lives of those you love better because you are in their lives"!

Because of your behavior your little girls are now in foster care; *frightened and wondering:* **"What did we do wrong? and there are lots of Daddys involved in this along with men and women of all ages!**

I Gently Said To Her,

"You *feel love* for your children but it appears that you do not have the ability to *deliver love...* the kind of love that makes their lives better because you are in their lives; like *nurturing, feeling a sense of safety and protection and the warmth that little children need"*

Again, I Challenged Her!

I said, "perhaps you love the drug dealer. You are making <u>his</u> life better!"

An Angry Response!

She said; "What do you mean I love the drug dealer? *I don't love the drug dealer!"*

This is Rough But Please Stay With Me!

I said; "Based on the fact that the Evidence Of Love is that you make the lives of the people you love better because you are in their lives, <u>The Evidence</u> is that you've been buying *drugs from the drug dealer* and making his life better. You are giving him the money that is meant for your children" Addiction is it's own hell!

I have found in my years of experience there are far more Daddys than Mommys along with the other men and women of all ages also suffer from alcohol and drug addiction.

I Gently Said To Her,

"Your behavior shows that you care more
about the excitement of the *"Hustle and the Chase"*,
the *drugs and the Drug Dealer* to whom you give the
money, than you do about your two little girls."

Your Behavior Says That !

Your behavior speaks so loud that
I can't hear what you're telling me
about how much love you feel
towards your two little girls."

Angrily She Said:
"That's Not So!"

She didn't like the *reality* of what she
was seeing. <u>Now</u> in her mind she was
saying "The *"Hustle and the Chase"*
or my little girls".

Here It Comes !
"I don't like what
you're saying! In fact,
I don't like you!"

Of Course Not !

*Reality of her addiction was breaking through.
She didn't like what she was seeing!*

She said; "I can have my two little
girls and the "Hustle and the Chase."
"I want my children and I don't have to give
up the "Hustle and the Chase" to have
them. "She was trying to convince herself.

She knew what I told her:
"You can't take the drugs out of the
"Hustle and the Chase any more than you
can take the wet out of the water."
She was thinking,
"I have to decide; If I stay with the
excitement of the "Hustle and the Chase",
then I can't have my little girls."

Then She Saw It !

"I can't take the drugs out of the excitement
of the "Hustle and the Chase." anymore
than I can take the wet out of the water,

but I can't live without the "Hustle and the Chase"!

Her desire that comes out of
her value system in addiction shows
that she actually values the "Hustle and the
Chase" more then her two little girls.
WHAT???
**Addiction is it's own hell and
She requires treatment and
treatment again if necessary!!!**

15

The children have a "Silent Scream" in their hearts and she wants the "Hustle and the Chase."

She said "If you take the "Hustle and the Chase" away, I will be in an emotional cage."

I said "Ever think that your two little girls are in an emotional cage? Mommy, Mommy where are you? When are you coming to get us?"

I was trying to Touch Her Heart and wake her up to Reality.

In life, in or out of addiction, people go for what they value the most! Like it or not, that's how it works.

In Alcohol or Drug Addiction There Is Help!

Help Through NA !
Help Through AA !
Help Through Treatment !

But You Have To Want It!

There Was Another Mother
who was also addicted to
alcohol & drugs and the
"Hustle and the Chase"

That Mother Said, in a moment of clarity

"I'm scared & frightened!"

She saw the reality of her behavior and how
it could cause her to lose her children.

Reaching Out, She Said:

"help me through this. My children
need me and I need them!"

You could see what she
valued most by her behavior.
With purpose in her heart
she went into treatment.

I Saw This Happen...

**I Saw This Happen the day CPS
brought a little boy and little
girl to see their mommy in rehab.
"Mommy! Mommy!"
They ran as fast as their little
feet could carry them into
her arms. Hugs and tears...
more tears and melting hearts.**

*Maybe because somebody reads
this and this is their story,
they may say to someone:
"help me through this"*

But if you don't try
you'll never know!

*And just today as I finished writting
this in my book and presented it in
a seminar, a woman in the third
row broke down in tears.*

**My words touched her heart.
Would she follow through?
I don't know!
Did my words touch your heart?
Will you follow through?**

**Again, It's Not Just About
Mommy, It's About DADDY Too!
Lots of Daddys!!!
Enter treatment and
enter it again if necessary!**

Fountains Of Understanding

"Triggers"
And Feelings

*You May Have Heard that the
"trigger" causes the relapse*

BUT WHAT IF THE "TRIGGER" DOES NOT CAUSE THE RELAPSE?

What the hell are you saying?

What If It Doesn't?
Hear me out!

There Are Many Books
But I read many people who had a Silent Scream in their heart
because they just couldn't understand the
way things were said, written or
presented to them and so they continue
to have difficulty maintaining their sobriety...
if that's you, what I offer here may help you.

The Trigger Does Not Cause The Relapse!

YOU can't cope with the feelings that the trigger produces so you, the alcoholic or addict, uses alcohol or drugs to make the feelings that the trigger produced "go away"

It's The Feelings

that you can't cope with, or live with so you drink or use drugs to make the feelings that the trigger produced "go away".

I'm Going To Say That Again !

What are you "nucking futs"? You said it two times and you're gonna say it again?

Yes, I am and no, I'm not *"nucking futs"*...

and Stay With Me, I'm gonna help you.

21

The Trigger Is Not The Issue!

It's your inability to cope with the feelings that the trigger caused that causes you to relapse to escape the feelings.

Again

you can't cope with the feelings that the trigger produces!

When you can't cope with the feelings... you use or drink to make the feelings that the Trigger produced go away.

That's How It Works!

Relapse!

The Dangerous Escape From FEELINGS That The Problems In Your Life Are Causing! The Feelings are Issue!

It Goes Like This, and stay with me!
She was 24...
She drank and used drugs "socially" with her true love.
...not at all uncommon these days.

One Day, He Left Her
For Another Young Lady!
She was hurt and devastated.

So then to escape her feelings
she began to drown them in
Alcohol and Drugs to
make them "go away".

For her a terrible **"IT"** had happened.
The **"IT"** was a painful and abrupt
abandonment by a man with whom she was
in love. She turned to alcohol and drugs
as a way of escaping her feelings.

That's how it goes... a natural affinity for
all too many to escape feelings that they don't like
instaed of processing them with someone.

Well, about a year later she was
"Twelve-Stepped" into the Fellowships of
AA and NA and with Help from people in the
Fellowships and with some therapy she worked her
way through it. She got it together and for
three wonderful years she was ok.
Life was beautiful.

Then one afternoon

**at the end of the three years with
the terrible "IT" well behind her...**
she was walking uptown on the west side of
Union Square in New York City, when a
guy passed by her going the other way.

**She never noticed him but as he
passed by her, she got a whiff
of the cologne he was wearing.
Her true love's cologne!!!**

For a moment there was a jolt!

**The scent of his cologne
was the "Trigger".**

*(Could be a guy and he got a scent of his
former girlfriend's perfume)*

The "Trigger"
Produced
The Feelings!!!!

The scent of the cologne brought
back the memories and all the feelings
that went with abandonment.

**It's the feelings that
you need help to cope with!**

Her feelings were going crazy. She
wanted to drink, to copp, to use
to make the feelings go away.
She couldn't cope with the feelings
that the "Trigger" had produced.

The "Terrible It"

**In her life her broken heart
was the terrible "IT Trigger"**

**What is the "Terrible
IT Trigger" in your life...**
that causes feelings that you
can't cope with and want to use over ?
broken relationships • bad marriage •
trouble with the law • rainy day • job •
debt • guilt • shame • memories • death

What?

**See something here
that applies to you?**

Stay with me...

You have to get help to cope with that or it's
going to cope with your behavior and you're going
to wind up relapsing!

You Can't Do It Alone!

**"You need and always will need
help to cope with the undesireable
feelings that any "Trigger" produces
that will cause you to relapse.
You have to get help to cope
with those feelings.
That's how it works...
Like it or not!!!**

**Meaningful Feedback From Others
Preferably in the Fellowships,**
is necessary to deal with the feelings that
are going on inside of you that cause you
to want to use and drink to make
those feelings "go away."
Painful Feelings caused by
too many bills · past mistakes · legal problems,
too much debt · trouble at home and work,
painful memories · medical problems...
See it? It's the feelings
that the trigger produces!

You Can't Do It Alone
if you try to manage the troubling
and disturbing feelings by yourself,
the troubling and disturbing feelings will
manage your behavior into relapse.
You Need Professional Help

Either you get help to help
you to cope with the troubling
feelings or you will relapse!

It doesn't take a Rocket Scientist
to understand this but it does take
sincerity of heart to use it in your
Life In Recovery.

Back To Her Story
From Pages 23, 24, & 25
And The Feelings That
The "Trigger" Produced

As the disturbing and troubling feelings came over her, she recalled seminars on "Triggers" and the problem of coping with those feelings that the "Trigger" produced.

She Got Help!

She got feedback from people in the Fellowships that she knew and trusted. They helped her to process her feelings so that her feelings didn't manage her behavior into drinking and using.

You Too Need To Get
Help To Avoid A Relapse.

The Question Is
Do You Care Enough
To Get The Help From
Your Sponsor Or A Friend
In The Fellowship?
Do <u>you</u> care enough?
The answer to that question can
determine your future

Your behavior & how you handle the feelings that any "Trigger" produces will absolutely play a role in creating the conditions and circumstances of your life and even the course of your life.

Day by day she processed the feelings down with help; constant feedback and understanding from her Sponsor and her friends in the Fellowship.

"A little at a time & stay tight with Fellowship People. Therapy is always an option if you need it" !

"The letter gets to where its going because the stamp sticks to it.

And if you stick to it, you will get to where you're going, which is to work through your problems and the feelings without using Alcohol or Drugs".

Help is just a phone call away!!!

28

In Keeping With What I've Written So Far...

on My YouTube page at:
"Recovery Another Approach"
you can see and
hear a very powerful
seminar called

Coping Skills In Addiction

It contains powerful graphics
and powerful real life stories
that drive the point home.

I presented it before
thousands of audiences

See and hear it now on
My YouTube page at:

Recovery Another Approach

AGAIN,
BECAUSE IT'S IMPORTANT!

When you show someone something from another angle they see it from another angle and they usually say "wow, I never looked at it that way".

That change in perception can enable someone to change the direction of their life.

If your life is going in the wrong direction this book shows you how making a change is within reach.

You Can Actually Frame The Course Of Someone's Entire Life With Words

Words of encouragement have produced Authors, Doctors, great Humanitarians and Business Leaders.

Words of destruction and Put-Downs and character assassinations also frame the course of a person's life and produce a self image that can become a lifetime of pain in a "prison without walls".

In my many years in the treatment field, many, many thousands of one-on-ones have lead me to believethat what I write about can be an underlying causativ factor in the use of alcohol and drugs and that factor needs treatment as part of the process in treating the alcohol and drug piece!

A constant flow of degrading words that are hurtful and demoralizing are a negative power of influence.

(Positive words and encouragement produce the opposite)

Both can and do frame the course of lives.

It Goes Like This!

Words that characterize someone as "bad",
or "less than desirable",
"not worth anything"
i.e.; you never do anything right, stupid,
klutzy, and more, have set people off into
lives of pain and heart sickness in that
"prison without walls" of which I speak.

And Other Words!

Never mind "not worth anything" or "you
never do anything right" or "stupid", but
words such as "fat", "ugly", and some
very bad vile words that I can't use here.

Not only words spoken

by adults to children but by spouses to
each other and because of the relentless
flow of such demeaning and hurtful words…
some people do turn to the use of Alcohol
and Drugs as a means of escaping that pain.

And they wear a "mask"…
a "mask" called a smile
to hide the pain that's
in their hearts!

They wear a "mask" but at night in bed
the mask comes off & the names they
were called become a "mirror" in which
they see themselves.

It Is True...

at night in bed the "mask" comes
off, and the demoralizing names
become a "mirror" in which
they see themselves.
And they cry. No, not with tears
but their heart cries and there is a
"Silent Scream" caused by the hurt and
the wounds from the verbal abuse.

The words of the
"Silent Scream" are:

"Won't somebody
love me?"
"Won't somebody
find me?"

Words
Are Like Seeds
and actually are seeds
i.e. Word Seeds

When spoken to someone
they are "Planted" in
their Inner Spirit.
A Person's Inner Spirit Is
"The Planting Field
Of Their Life"

**I've Met People
whose Self Worth is so poor**
from the demoralizing and destructive
"Put Down Words" spoken to them that
because of the lingering pain and memories
**that they actually do seek
escape in alcohol & drugs.**

**Can you believe I made <u>that</u> statement
"when we all know" that they're just
using alcohol and drugs as an
excuse to get drunk or to get "high"?
I'm being facetious here**

**What if
those things
are not excuses?
Do I dare say that?**

**What if they are
underlying causativ factors
in the use of alcohol
and drugs that
requires treatment?**

34

Sticks and Stones

will break your bones and the bones will
heal, but the Put Downs & the demoralizing
names and memories can go around the
canyons of your mind for a lifetime.

I Said Upfront,

Words of Encouragement have produced
Authors, Doctors, Teachers, Scientists
Artists, great Humanitarians
and Business Leaders.

Words Of Destruction

and Put-Downs also frame the course
of a person's life and produce a Self Image
that can become a lifetime of pain.
I've seen it again and again.

There are sometimes unspoken words of
destruction and demoralization directed at
us by someone or a group of people
and "no one said anything"?
Ever been on the receiving end of the
"deep freeze" the "cold shoulder"?

It's Called The

"The Violence of Silence"

It hurts and it sends the message loud
and clear that goes right through you

Fountains Of Understanding

**What I am presenting here may
well be a major contributing
"underlying causative factor"
in the continued use of
Alcohol and Drugs by many.**

**The underlying causativ factor
is not an excuse, it's a reality
that has to be taken into
consideration and treated!!!
Treatment on your part is needed!**

Many use Alcohol and Drugs
as a means of escaping themselves and
escaping the pain of poor self image and
low self worth, and <u>lots of things</u> that are
well hidden behind the smile that they wear.

**To validate this factor is not
to give anyone an excuse to
"cop out" as a victim.**

**Validation of this is about
helping those who struggle with
this not to "drop out" but to
seek help in treatment!
I'm speaking to YOU the target
audience of this book!**

The Unspoken Word Speaks In Many Forms Of Behavior.

Ever been "dissed" without a word ever being spoken? Ignored? Passed by as though you weren't there? The look of disgust perhaps sent to you with a passing glance?
You feel it go right through you. You do!

You know it happened, and no one said anything.

And if you bring it up, and you may have done that and heard the response
"You're just being paranoid"

Hey! Listen!
Behavior is it's own language.

It can break the heart and the spirit of a person as cruelly as hurtful spoken words.
There's no shame, you are not alone!
Seek treatment! Seek help!

His Name Was "Bobby"

He was a soft spoken little 4 year old boy.
When you looked at him
you just wanted to hug him.

Little Bobby's Story
Goes Like This,

His Mother had been sick for some time.
Then, shortly after Bobby's fourth birthday,
his Mother died. Quite a trauma for a little
4 year old boy, wouldn't you say? There
were questions inside of him. Questions
that a 4 year old couldn't put into words.

About A Year After
His Mother Died,

His handsome young Daddy got him a
new Mommy. She was young and good
looking like his Daddy & she was pregnant.

Bobby's Daddy And His
New Mommy Sat Him Down

and explained that he would soon have
a little baby sister and that "Julie"
would be her name.

4 Months Later little
Baby "Julie" Was Born

She was the center of his new Mommy's
attention. And she was also the center
of his Daddy's attention too.

Baby Julie Was The Center Of Attention All The Time!
Bobby Felt Left Out!

(on the outside looking in)
His Daddy and his new Mommy's behavior
towards Little Julie was speaking
loud and clear to him.

And Then,

Little Bobby spoke words
to himself inside himself.
(It's called "self talk")
"They love her more than me,
I don't count anymore."
Their behavior was
translated into words.

Bobby's Heart Cried!

It's not always safe to cry with tears,
<u>So Your Heart Cries.</u>

Again And Important...

This <u>is not</u> about blame or being a victim.
It's about overcoming all of this & becoming
who you want to be without the need for
your using alcohol and drugs.

One day Little Bobby told his Daddy how he felt!

His Daddy assured him that they loved him as much as little Julie.

Done !!!

"That Took Care Of That"

But Not Really !

Not Really At All !

Their continued behavior toward Little baby Julie did not bear out the words of reassurance that his Daddy had spoken to him

Their Behavior Spoke Quite Loudly!

The sense of loss in Bobby's Heart grew ever more painful!

He so wanted them to show him the "Behavior Of Love" and caring that his spirit hungered for: the kind of love that they showed little baby Julie. No mystery to this.

One Winter's Day
I was headed for the beach

I took little Bobby with me.
There's a "quiet wonder" to the beach
in winter. That day a soft and gentle
snow was falling.

As We Walked Bobby Asked;
"you know what's
a Real Bad Word?"

I asked:
"What's a Real Bad Word?"

"STUPID" he said

"My new Mommy calls me "Stupid"
and it's a Real Bad Word You Know."

What makes "Stupid"
a real bad word is that it hurts
and makes one's heart cry.

Stupid isn't just a word.
Stupid is a "Seed."

Words can be and are "Seeds!"
ie; "Word Seeds"

Word Seeds

The "Word Seeds" spoken to you <u>or at you</u>
that deal with good or bad characterization;
when "Planted" in <u>your</u> spirit produce what's
in them. It's called "Genetics". The "Word Seeds"
produce what's in them the very same way that
seeds produce when the farmer plants
his seeds in the field.

It Goes Like This;

In the farmer's field are both the heat from
The sun and the moisture from the rain.
The same thing occurs in you when either
good or bad characterization "Word Seeds"
are spoken and planted inside of you
In "The Planting Field" of your life.

**I am speaking of Destructive
Words here. "STUPID"!
She Called Him.**

**The <u>Hurt</u> that "Stupid" caused
in his heart was the "<u>Heat</u>"
and then his heart cried and
that was the "<u>Moisture</u>"**

**The "Stupid Seed" that she planted
in him opened and brought
forth "Stupid" in a little boy's life.**

That's How It works!!!

Look At This !!!

When you receive "Characterization Word Seeds" in your spirit, spoken to you by someone they really do get inside of you with their genetics that is in them.

Then you "Water Them"

The characterization that is in the words good or bad play a role in creating your self image and your self worth as you live life and interface with others.

I Water Them?
How Do I Water Them?

The "Characterization Word Seeds" that are spoken to you go around the canyons of your mind and you repeat them to yourself.

That's "Watering Them"!

In your case, as in little Bobby's case, you "water" the words by unconsciously speaking them over and over to yourself in your mind. They become a part of your Belief System.

It goes beyond the "Seed Word" "Stupid" in the lives of many. Believe me!
It went way beyond that with little Bobby in his house and maybe with you in your house.

Stay With Me !

43

Nothing wrong with "Watering" the words and Entertaining them but <u>which</u> or <u>what</u> "Characterization Word Seeds" <u>are you</u> or <u>have you</u> been Watering or Entertaining?

**I said,
As I began,**
"You can frame the course
of someone's life with words"

Words of Encouragement have produced
Authors, Doctors, Teachers, Scientists,
Artists, great Humanitarians,
and business leaders.

Words of destruction and "put-downs"
also frame the course of a person's life
and they produce a poor self-image that
can become a lifetime of pain
in a "Prison Without Walls."

**No man or women will ever
rise above the image that
they have of themselves!
If your self image is poor, think
about that! There is help for this
in treatment!**

Little Bobby
might have said:

" Mirror, Mirror, on the wall.
The Mirror isn't there at all.
The "Little Stupid" in the Mirror that I see.
He's not in the Mirror.
The "Little Stupid" <u>is</u> <u>in</u> <u>me</u>".
I project the Image of "Little Stupid"
in the Mirror from the "Word Seeds"
that were "planted" inside of me.

Get That?

Now How About You?

"Mirror, Mirror, on the wall.
The Mirror isn't there at all.
The Shame in the Mirror that I see.
It's not in the Mirror.
The Shame is in me".
"I project it there from the "Word Seeds"
<u>that were "Planted"</u> inside of me".

THINK! BY WHO AND WHEN!

**You're Right!
I'm "Watering them
and they're becoming part
of my belief system about myself"
I See It!**

Look At This !

**Mirror, Mirror, on the wall.
The Mirror isn't there at all.
The "Never Amount To Anything"
in the Mirror that I see.
He or she is not in the Mirror!
The "Never Amount To Anything"
IS IN ME!**

**But, I Say, No Way !
I Say, I Say,
You Are Just Having A Little
Difficulty In The Process Of
Changing And Succeeding !**

**If you're not in the process
of changing andsucceeding,
and if that is not so,
why are you reading
this book?**

As you read the "Outside The Box" things
in this book you are in the process of
changing many of the things that you thought!
And so you are succeeding at changing!

**Think About That!
It's A Process! You not only have
to be in it but you have
to want to be in it!
Treatment is
part of that process!**

The Process Of Becoming!!

**"The Process Of Becoming"
is the process of becoming
who it is that you want to become
and will become and will be as you
succeed in making the change.**

You play the major role in who it is you
become based on the power of influence
that you are under as you live by both
the words that you water in the
"Planting Field Of Your Life" and the
Power of Influence that you allow
yourself to be under and around.
I.e. words and people
Read that again!

Back To Little Bobby,
As Bobby Grew Up,

in response to the barrage of words that hurt
him, he hurt back at his Mother and Father. He
did that with very wild and crazy ass behavior.

The Problem Was...

Bobby had <u>unknowingly</u> turned the desire to
hurt them back, in on himself, with wild his
and crazy ass behavior. He was young and
had no idea that in what he was doing to
hurt them, he was in reality hurting himself.
That's Bobby back then,
What about you now?

Is It Possible ?

Could the hurts, the words, the wounds
and memories from those hurtful
characterizations, or even the hurt that
you feel by their "not loving you",
go around the canyons of <u>your</u> mind?

Absolutely!!!

It's True!

**The Feelings, The Hurt's,
The Bad Memories, And
The Characterization
Words, Don't Really
Go Away.**

They "go away" temporarily...
when you are high or when you are
drunk. They only "go away" for a little
while and then the memories, the feelings,
and the other stuff comes back.

They Come Back
stronger then ever and the damage that you
do to yourself by your drinking and drugging
and crazy ass behavior hurts You again.

**And Tell Me!
What In The Hell Are
You Doing To Yourself
When Help Is Available
with nothing more
than a phone call?**

Now, Back To Bobby

Little Bobby was subject to more then the word "stupid".
There was a constant barrage of put downs in the home.
I mean some bad stuff.

Bobby Became A "Garbage Dump" For "Garbage Words"

As he grew up with the hurts, he hurt back.
And the gentle soft spoken boy was turned
into a loud, angry, and broken boy, under
the wounds of the destructive words,
but no one saw this that I write about here.

Break Here For A Moment...
Some people would say and
have said that I am making
too much of this.

What I Write About Is Real
and may be what I call an
"Underlying Causative Factor"
in the use of alcohol and drugs.
and that underlying causativ
factor needs treatment as part
of treating addiction

Listen, Hey,
If it doesn't apply, let it fly.
But please don't shut me out !

This That I Write About

applies to more people than most realize.
Lots of life forming and damaging words
are spoken behind closed apartment doors
in the city and behind the blue and green
doors and manicured lawns in houses
in the suburbs.

Those Who Suffer

from the hurts of which I speak about
here look for approval. The heart hungers
for approval. It is a Powerful, Basic, Human, Need
and when it is unmet, many seek and find
the wrong kind of approval in the
alcoholic and drug world and to hurt back
for the hurts they received.

Back To Bobby ...

Over time because of the wild and crazy
ass behavior he entered into, to hurt his
Mother and Father, Bobby's Father lost
patience and joined in on the word blitz.
The destructive put downs and demoralizing
characterizations directed at him as he was
growing up were giving Bobby a self image
from which he wanted to escape.

**It's a vicious cycle & this is not
about blame or being a victim,
its about overcoming this stuff
without using Alcohol & Drugs.**

At 14 Years Old
In This Game of Hurt
and Hurt Back, Bobby had
Already Entered the World of
Alcohol And Drug Use.

Bobby found that the alcohol and drugs took him out of himself for a period of time. He found approval in the world of alcohol & drug use along with other kids his age who were fighting their "shadows" as he was fighting his "shadows".

"Shadows"

The shadows are the demoralizing words and the hurts and the painful memories to which you can't and sometimes <u>don't dare</u> put words. The memories and the hurts lie somewhere in

the "Shadows"
in Your Heart.

This is not only true of parents to children but of spouse to spouse as well!

Follow this with me!

The Author of this story is unknown.
A busy business man had come home
from work on the railroad. It was a hot
summer night, no AC on the railroad.
He got home exhausted and tired.

When he got home he made himself a light dinner.

and was sitting in the den reading a magazine.
Along came his little 4-year-old-son.
"Daddy, want to play with me?"

"Not now, Daddy's reading"
His son kept at it. He wasn't giving up!

At That Moment,

his Father turned the page in
the magazine that he was reading.
There was a 2 page ad for an airline.
On the left hand page it showed the perks
and pictures of destinations. On the right
hand page was a map of the world. It
showed the routes of the airline.

So his father tore the map page out of the
magazine that he was reading and
showed it to his little 4-year-old son &
said "Look, this is a map of the world".

After He Showed The Map
To His 4-Year-Old Son
he tore the map into pieces
and gave it to his little Son.

And Said: "Now you go get tape
from your Mommy and you put the
map back together. When you
put it back together correctly,
Daddy will play with you".

His Daddy

had no problem because his little
4-year-old was not going to get
the map back together correctly , so he
wouldn't have to play with him.

Ten minutes later
loud and exuberant,
Here came his
4-year-old son:
"I did it! I did it!"
"Now play with
me Daddy !"

He Handed the Taped
Page to His Father that
He had Put Together!

It Was Not Neat,
But It Was Right !

"How Did You Do That?"
His Father Asked.

The Boy Looked Up
At His Father And Said:
"Look Daddy! On the other
side of the map of the world
there is a picture of a man".

"See Daddy, I put the man
together and the whole
world came together! "

How About It?
Are You Ready To Put
Your World Together?

This book may
help you to do that!!
Read On!!

At The Start Of This Book I Said:
"You can frame the course of someone's life with words".
The Words In This Book And In The Self Help Fellowships...

Whatever self-help fellowships you choose to participate in for your life can and will help you to reframe and redirect the course of your life; if you really want it and you **listen with your heart.**

Also the words spoken in the Fellowship of a Church as well. Yes, in a Church Fellowship if you so choose. The words there can also help you to frame and reframe and redirect the course of <u>your</u> life.

This in addition to the AA and NA Fellowships since the alcoholic and addict who continues to have difficuty maintaining their sobriety

Words Heal Hurts
Words Heal Wounds
Words Heal Memories
Words get inside of you and play a role in your destiny!

IT'S True !

**In all of The Fellowships of
which I speak
there are Words of
Acceptance and
Encouragement for you!**

**In The Fellowships
there are Words of
Sincere Caring for you!**

**In The Fellowships
there are Words of
Guidance & Understanding
to help redirect your life !**

**In The Fellowships
there are Words of
Healing for your life!**

**And Those Words
will get in and begin to grow
in the "Planting Field"
Of Your Life...**

This Is What Happens!
Words of Encouragement!
Those words of Guidance!
Words of Understanding!
Those words of Healing!
that will be planted in the
"Planting Field Of Your Life",
replacing what's inside of you:
Bringing
Healing To The
"Shadows"
In Your Heart.

A Little At A Time...
A little at a time...
A little at a time...

Little Drops Of Water
and little grains of sand,
when put together,
make a mighty ocean and
a very pleasant land.

A Little Bit Here
and a little bit there!
Words here, Words there,
Words that help you to
redirect your life

To the Author From The Reader
you said this is for people who have been
in and out of AA, NA, Rehab,
and even Jail.
They already know a lot of this stuff!

**However, they might not have ever seen
them or looked at things quite this way.
When you see things from a different
angle, you really do see them differently.**

**As I Presented different way of
seeing things in my thousands
of seminars, many said "I never
looked at it that way" and said
"I never even thought of that!"
Many Returned
to AA and NA, Rehab and to Church
with New Understanding
and a new "Mind Set"**

A Spark Was Ignited!!

**All of my Seminars
are available to you on**

YouTube at:

"Recovery Another Approach"

Hey! Almost Forgot About "Little Bobby"

Last I heard, Bobby is 30 years old.
He is in the Fellowships. He is! He found
an older man there who is his sponsor;
who mentors him, who cares about him,
and who encourages him.

It Was What He Needed
in the process of putting
his shattered life together.

He Has A Lady In His Life.
They tell me she loves him.
She admires him as well as loving him.
She encourages him and he encourages her.

Bobby Has A New Life

This new life for him started with his
understanding of "Words Seeds" and the
"Planting Field Of His Life". Bobby wants
to be an Alcohol and Drug Counselor.

He understands that it is not just about alcohol and drugs. He understands that some also need healing of the "Shadows In Their Heart".

60

Bobby

**Found A New Life
In The Fellowships
Speaking of Fellowships,
Bobby Joined
A Church Fellowship.**

**Bobby Is In The Music
Ministry Of His Church.
Bobby Plays
The Lead Trumpet.**

Now See If You
Can Grasp This!

**Somewhere
Along The Way,
Bobby's Heart Heard
"The Trumpet Sound For Him"
and he went into treatment!**

**After Reading This
That I Presented Here
Did Your Heart Hear
The Trumpet
Sound For You?**

**Someone's Heart Did!
And they are going into treatment!**